ALL YOU W

D

SUMEET SHARMA

New Dawn

NEW DAWN
An imprint of Sterling Publishers (P) Ltd.
A-59 Okhla Industrial Area, Phase-II, New Delhi-110020.
Tel: 6912677, 6910050, 6916165, 6916209
Fax: 91-11-6331241 E-mail: ghai@nde.vsnl.net.in
www.sterlingpublishers.com

All You Wanted to Know About Dowsing

ISBN 81 207 2274 4

Reprint 2002

Published by Sterling Publishers Pvt. Ltd., New Delhi-110016.
Lasertypeset by Vikas Compographics, New Delhi-110029.
Printed at Prolific Incorporated, New Delhi-110020.

Contents

This book is dedicated to Shri Debu Ghosh, my psychic Guru who attuned me to the 5th dimension

Acknowledgements

I am thankful to Shri Debu Ghosh for teaching me the fundamentals of Dowsing, my wife, Lalitha, for editing this book my son, Samrat, for helping me in typing and the staff of Seamak Group and Sterling Publishers Pvt. Ltd., in bringing forth this publication, and my friends who were already into Dowsing since several years.

Preface

When I met Debu Ghosh from Mumbai who is into psychic healing since the last 30 years, I knew that something was in store for me to raise my consciousness to higher levels of understanding.

This is exactly what happened with me when I did his psychic healing course which attuned me to the 5th or PSI dimension where all the knowledge beyond earthly wisdom exists and is also known as the *Akashic* records. The course also connected me to healing guides and made me a 100 per cent clairvoyant. I am now able to scan auras and reveal to people, psychically the blocks in advances.

I also started receiving many subtle information during my meditations. I was able to tap into people's subconscious in the alpha state of mind. This skill has been developed by me under the able instructions of my guides.

Dowsing is an advanced science that is yet to be recognised in India. In the USA, Canada, Australia and some parts of Europe extensive research has been carried out in this field.

This is just a basic book channelled by my guides on the day-to-day use of the pendulum to make you nearly 95 per cent accurate most of the time.

History of Dowsing

Everyman takes the limit of his own field of vision for the limits of the world.

-Aristotle

The word 'dowsing' is derived from the Greek word *deuden* (to declare). It means searching for anything by projecting an intention of what is desired and receiving confirmation or non-confirmation feedback through the body using an instrument. It is a form of clairvoyance, the ability to see at any given moment what is happening elsewhere.

Dowsing is also referred to as 'divining' which is derived from the word 'divinus'. Divining is a spiritual practice and the success or the outcome of the divining depends on the divine state of mind.

Dowsing is not a new science but has been in existence since time immemorial and this is revealed from the paintings of 6000 BC wherein a human-like figure is seen holding a forked stick like a Y rod to search for water. A Chinese emperor, Yu, in 2000 BC was a good dowser who travelled all over the world to demonstrate his talent.

Even in the *Bible,* there is a subtle mention of dowsing tools used by Moses. In the 16th century and the Renaissance period treatise and coins show dowsers at work. In the Bergbau Museum at Bochem, Germany, there is a 15th century Meissen figurine of a dowser, clad in the uniform of a miner holding a forked stick.

Earlier dowsing was mainly used for divining water which is dealt with in the following chapter. A dowser was a respected person in society and anyone wishing to dig a well without consulting a dowser was considered a fool. Even in our country our forefathers took the help of a dowser before attempting to dig wells.

Water diviners are gifts of god to mankind as He knew that man will not be able to survive without water. Generally, I do not encourage my students to do water divining on a professional basis as it will deprive the gifted diviners of their livelihood and the special psychic sense with which they are born.

Dowsing was actively used till the Victorian era. When scientific research started, the concept of dowsing could not be demonstrated and repeated as per the demands of the scientific community.

It was after World War II that dowsing received renewed attention because one could search for lost items, oil reserves, metal ores, missing persons, criminals and even locations of air plane crash sites.

Today, the modern dowser determines exactly where the underground water lines run, which is beyond the reach of any sophisticated machine, and it can accurately pinpoint its depth, including the water flow rate. The recent trend is not to even use a pendulum.

In 1961, in the state of Vermont, a non-profit organisation with 100 charter members called American Society of Dowsers, Inc. was formed. This is a premier organisation that gives information on dowsing.

Once a French Nobel laureate said, "We must accept dowsing as a fact. It is useless to work experiments merely to prove its existence it exists. What is needed is its development for better human understanding."

What is Dowsing?

A pessimist is someone who when confronted with two unpleasant choices selects both.

-Anon

The dictionary definition of dowsing is "using paranormal process to make a discovery, using a pendulum like tool and rods made out of metal or natural substance".

Dowsing or divining is one of the oldest sciences being rediscovered and holds promise for at least the next three decades to come. It is one of the most puzzling and interesting techniques which can get you hooked or even addicted to.

While dowsing we use an external tool like an ordinary pendulum as shown in Figure 1 which swings to give answers to most questions bothering us in our daily life. It can also be very handy in finding objects, water, selection of medicines, etc. This is what we are going to learn about in the subsequent chapters.

The pendulum is directly connected to our intuitive centre and it moves on its own without any physical effort on our part to give answers from our unconscious mind.

An Ordinary Pendulum

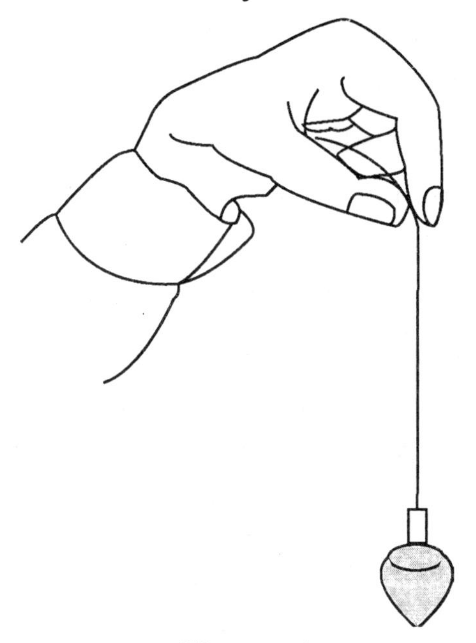

Figure 1

We have three types of mind:

- Conscious mind
- Subconscious mind

- Unconscious or superconscious mind

The conscious mind is our natural brain or say the left side of the brain that is fed with enough information from childhood to be analytical and linear in all our approaches. The bad news is that it is only 7 per cent of the total mind. All our earthly knowledge perceived by the five senses is stored in this mind.

The subconscious mind is the mind with submerged consciousness that is contributed by the right side of the brain. It is non-rational, non-linear and carries memories of our past lives. This is what makes us react to situations. All happy or sad moments, traumatic events, emotions and fear remain in the subconscious mind. This is 38 per cent of the total mind capacity. We thus condition the mind even before birth. This also explains some of the birth disorders, which is not explained by current medical knowledge.

The unconscious or super conscious mind is 55 per cent of the mind capacity. This mind is connected to higher dimensions in a mysterious way wherein the entire universal knowledge is accessible provided one raises his consciousness to that level either through training or spiritual growth.

Unconscious mind is connected to our intuition or the sixth sense that always does things for our good. Intuition is our greatest friend and inner voice of God and we must always listen to what it has to say to us.

Dowsing tools are connected to the superconscious mind which can be partly understood by various scientific theories written till now.

How Does Dowsing Work?

In theory there should not be much difference between theory and practice but in practise there often is.

-Anon

Many theories have been applied to explain dowsing by using scientific theories and well-known scientific principles.

All scientific hypothesis is believed to be true till it is replaced by another superior hypothesis. When Copernicus discovered and declared that the earth is not the centre of all the planets and it is the earth with all the other planets which go round the sun, he was hanged. The biggest enemy of the scientists are the scientists themselves.

Some of the possible explanation given are:

- **Radar Principle** : A radar sends a signal to the object which is deflected and sensed again by it to give the distance. Similarly while water divining, one can find the depth of water below the ground level using a pendulum. According to this theory, some kind of signal is sent by the pendulum to the water body and received back to make it move. However, this theory fails when we ask subjective questions or those related to the future, where there is no object involved there is only abstract situation or decision.

- **Atamic or Soul Force** : According to the Hindu theory there is an *atamic* force behind the movement of the pendulum or our higher self might be guiding the pendulum or according to the occult science our guides might be giving physical answers to our questions. Beyond our physical plane of existence there is a dimension of different time and space not understood fully by science whereas mystics like Zen masters, Yogis, Buddhist monks and Lamas completely believe in the mystery because they work in this dimension most of the times. Our unconscious mind is connected to this dimension. A Zen master would perhaps ask you, "What is the sound of one hand clapping?" Although this sounds illogical, your thinking process gets activated.

- **Subconscious Mind**: Some people tend to believe that it is the subconscious mind which makes the pendulum move. It is true for a new dowser, but a skilled dowser would know how to overcome this interference also. The school of thought here is that all the questions have an answer in the subconscious. We will see in the subsequent chapters that questions asked about situations not yet encountered in our life also receive correct answers.

- **Hologram Principle**: This is the most satisfactory principle based on the principle of oneness and interconnectedness. Suppose a picture of a rose is taken by an ordinary camera and its negatives cut into several pieces and then developed, naturally all the developed photos will be cut. Now if a holographic camera is used and its negative is cut into several pieces and laser beam is passed through each piece, each will resemble the original as a whole. This proves the microcosm and macrocosm principle of mini universe in all of us and that there is no difference between humans, animals and matter and in the manner we perceive things. We perceive externally what we are internally. If we have goodness in us we will see goodness everywhere.

Hence are we part of the whole or whole of the part?

PSI Factor and Hologram Principle

Science is below the mind, spirituality and consciousness is above the mind.

-Sathya Sai Baba

Parapsychology has two challenges of psychic powers' existence. Assuming this to be true then what is the basis of our beliefs in logical explanation and scientific experiment being followed for so many years? We have tuned our minds to become highly logical and scientific and thereby missing the glory of the universe created by God.

Anything is termed scientific if the experiment or theory can be repeated and demonstrated giving the same result every time. However, all occult sciences are in the dimension of mystery and would seldom give the same or consistent results that can be measured in physical plane.

Science has discovered X-rays over the past two centuries. They are short high frequency waves and at other end long low frequency waves such as radio waves from distant planets. All our modern gadgets made available for home use are based on these principles.

We fail to understand that there are subtle energies in this universe which are not measurable by any known instrument. Science is not inventing anything actually it is only rediscovering what is already present in the universe.

We perceive two dimensions and three dimensions easily as objects belong to either of the two and if we add the factor of time that cannot be perceived by human senses, we get the fourth dimension. Time is a relative factor and subjective too hence each person reacts to his own perception of time. This was Einstein's Theory of Relativity which explained many concepts like electro-magnetism that could not be explained by Newtonian physics as it was still stuck to the three dimension coordinate, i.e., x, y and z axis.

The fifth dimension is the PSI factor that is formed by the intersection of human consciousness and these four dimensions are directly perpendicular to these coordinates.

At the PSI dimension, information travels beyond the natural laws under current knowledge. This explains ESP, Astral travel and Telepathy. Nostradamus, Edgar

Cayce, Dr Carl Yung and many others had their mind directly attuned to PSI dimension.

One of the peculiar experiments done in physics is the behaviour of the subatomic particles.

Experiment 1:

Two particles, electron and positron, i.e., matter and anti-matter when collided created two photons (light particles) which sped off in two different directions as shown in Figure 2. Photon A did not possess spin or velocity till it was noted by the observer that it can act both like a wave or a particle (relativity).

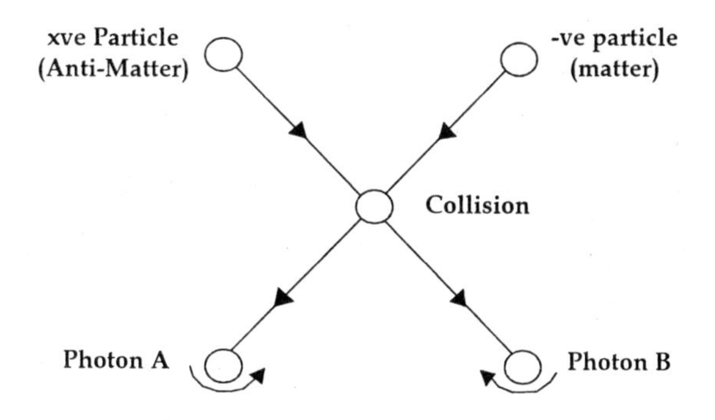

Figure 2

When observed it starts spinning and photon B also does the reverse of spinning in the opposite direction regardless of the distance and no connection whatsoever. Photon B instantly knows what A is doing. This explains clairvoyance and other psychic phenomenon.

Experiment 2 :

A research team led by physicist Allain Aspect, discovered under certain circumstances that subatomic particles were able to instantly communicate with each other regardless of distance separating them. These particles are known as "Eidolons" which are infinitely interconnected and that is the essence of the entire universe.

The above are just brief details of a very sophisticated experiment done. Here we can see the clear violation of the Einstein's law that states that nothing travels faster than light, in other words rendering the concept of time as null and void.

Physicist Dr David Bohm, from the University of London later reconfirmed that objective reality is an illusion despite its apparent solidity and in essence the universe is a hologram.

The whole universe appears to be a dynamic web of inseparable energy patterns, an inseparable whole, which always includes the observer in an essential way.

In his book, *The Implicate Order* Dr Bohm has made a mention that laws of physics cannot be understood by science by dividing the world into several parts. This book also explains the hologram concept that every piece is an exact representation of the whole and each piece can be used to reconstruct the entire hologram again.

In 1971, Dr Dennis Gabor received the Nobel Prize for constructing the first hologram proving Dr Bohm's concepts.

Science tends to understand things only in a linear fashion. We cannot describe a simple daily experience in words because we use words in a linear fashion. Meditation is one way of transcending the linear mind and allowing connectedness of all things to become an experiential reality.

These concepts are not new as the Vedic philosophy says, *Isa Vasyam Idam Sarvam Ethinchat Jaganth Jagath* meaning "all is god and pervaded by god".

Getting Started with the Pendulum

The biggest problem can be solved when it is small.

-Lao Tse

To understand subsequent exercises it would be better to have a pendulum in your hand as it will be easy to practice then and there. If you do not have a perfect pendulum then any heavy metal or even a wooden bob would do to start with. [Figure 3(a)] Pendulums made of crystal, wood or metal would all serve the same purpose.[Figure 3(b)]

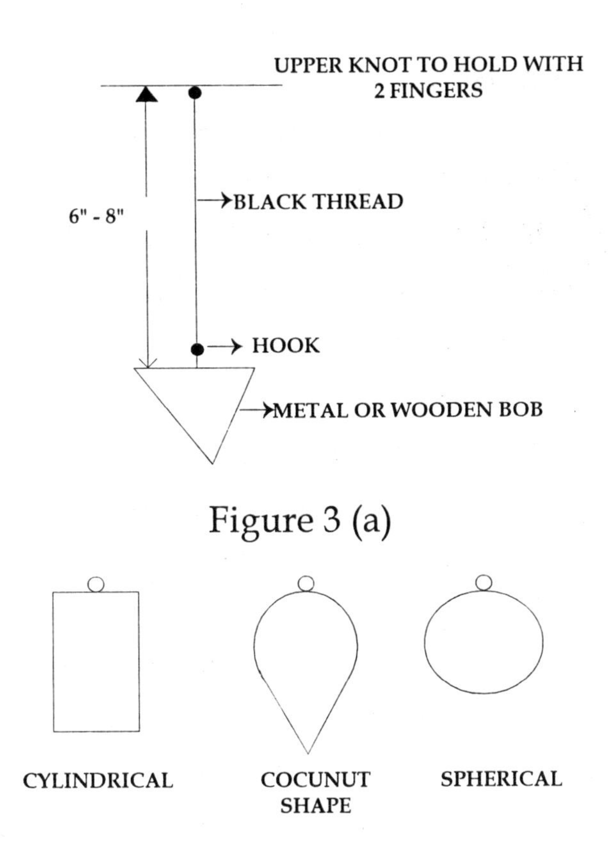

Figure 3 (a)

Figure 3 (b) Other forms of Bob

Exercise 1 :

Hold your pendulum in the hand with two fingers(either thumb and index finger or thumb and middle finger) and ask the pendulum, "Show me your search position." Generally the pendulum moves clockwise and anticlockwise after a gap of a few seconds it may totally remain still, anything is fine.

Next question is, "Show me your 'Yes' position." It may show Y-axis vertically or X-axis horizontally or anticlockwise/ clockwise. If it shows it is fine otherwise you can programme the 'Yes' swing for Y-axis by swinging the pendulum in

Y-axis for at least 10 times and then repeat mentally or verbally to the pendulum that, "This is your 'Yes' position."

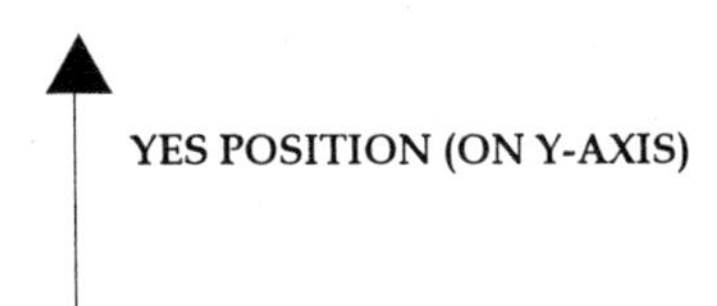

For the 'No' position, programme horizontally on X-axis by swinging it 10 times and repeat mentally or verbally to the pendulum that, "This is your 'No' position."

Similarly you can programme for the anticlockwise movement by swinging the pendulum 10 times and repeating mentally or verbally to the pendulum, "This is your Wrong Question swing". And clockwise movement for "I do not want to answer this question "swing.
Now your pendulum is programmed for use.

So get set for an Exciting Adventure in Dowsing

Let us revise the swings:

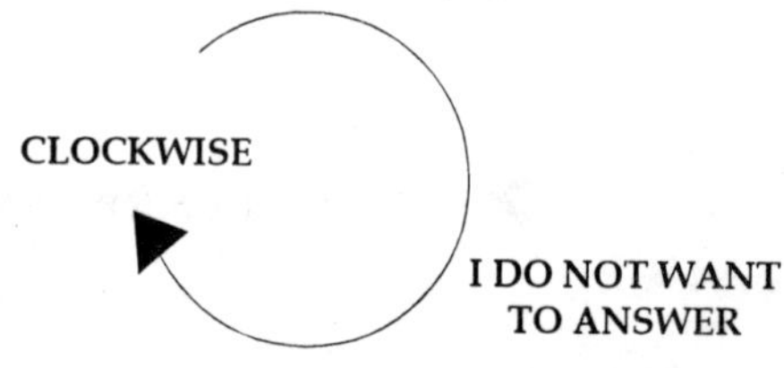

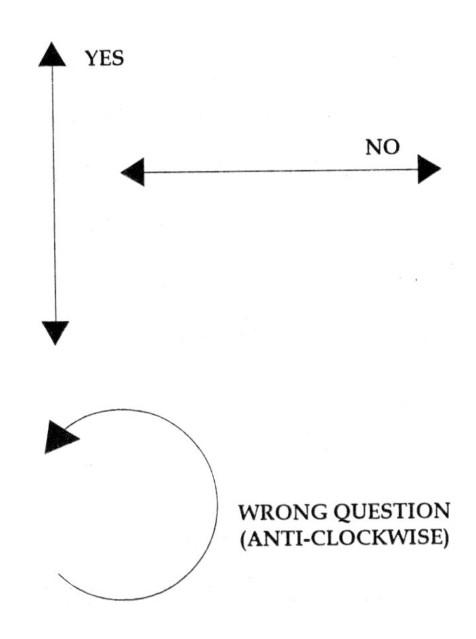

Now ask the pendulum "Is my name... (your name). If the pendulum gives 'Yes' swing, then it is fine. Otherwise programme the pendulum again. Ask an opposite question of 'Yes' and note the swing.

For instance you can ask, "Is my name... (not your actual name)". This is to check the programme.

If the pendulum gives feeble swings say, "Magnify Swing" and the swings would become stronger.

Exercise 2 :

Three coin test

Take two coins of similar denomination, like a one-rupee coin, and one coin of two-rupee. When we place the two similar coins apart and place the pendulum in between the coins, the pendulum will swing in 'Yes' swing automatically and when we remove

remove one of the similar coins and place a dissimilar coin then the pendulum will automatically swing in 'No' direction.

Exercise 3 :

Guessing the names in closed chits

Take small strips of paper and write down the names of all your family members and fold the chit and mix them thoroughly.

If you have ten chits in all, take one chit and ask, "Is this chit having so and so name written on it?"

Note 'Yes' or 'No' swing, then open the chits and note down right or wrong answer.

Repeat the same with all the chits and note down the percentage of right and wrong names indicated by the pendulum. Even if you get 50 per cent of the answer right you can be assured that you are grooming to become a good dowser. This is a very effective exercise and can be done with two people also.

Variations of this exercise is the tossing of the coin. Ask your friend to toss the coin and check with the pendulum for heads or tails and note the swing of 'Yes' and 'No'.

Guessing the cards: Place ten playing cards, ranging from numbers 1–10, shuffle them thoroughly and check with the pendulum for 'Yes' or 'No' swing by asking questions regarding the numbers 1,2,3,...?

You can add spades, hearts, diamonds and clubs to selected cards and check. By regular practice you can become an expert dowser.

Some Useful Tips to Become a Good Dowser

- Do not dowse in a hurry or when you are in a bad mood.
- Do not get discouraged when you do not get correct answers. No dowser has got 100 per cent correct answers. There is a technical reason for that which is discussed in the next chapter.
- Dowse in privacy or in the presence of people with sound understanding. Even the observer affects the experiments (explained in detail in the next chapter).

- Do not show off your dowsing skills in parties or social gatherings unless and until you are sure about your dowsing skills. If you sport your amateurish skills and do not obtain good and correct answers you may get discouraged.
- Dowse for others only when you are at least habitually getting upto 80 per cent right answers as per exercises given earlier.
- Do not dowse for questions which already have logical answers. Dowsing should be practised for an answer you need to know about things that have

more than one option and helps you to take a final decision. First arrive at all logical answers.(We shall discuss it in the next chapter).

- Dowser should learn to be composed and should completely surrender to the higher energies.

Why not 100 per cent Answers?

We may invent the elixir of immortality, but it will take forever to prove it.

-Anon

The best dowser has also obtained only 96-98 per cent correct answers. We need to understand two important laws of human psyche.

1st Law: The perceiver pollutes the perception of what is being perceived.

2nd Law: Prejudice affects the present that infects the future.

The perceiver or the dowser must understand that the answers of the pendulum come from PSI dimension where linearity has no meaning. Hence if your pendulum is giving 'No' answer for your most expected answer 'Yes' then it is either for your highest good or you have not done your homework correctly.

So let us take an example of Mr X who has applied for a job in several companies and has received two appointment letters from two different organisations of equal standing. Let us see how he takes the various logical steps.

1. Background of each company, years of standing, products, quantum raise and perks. Give marks for each point considered.
2. Do I have to travel far everyday and leave home and family?
3. Are there frequent transfers involved?
4. Do I have to bribe people, if so can I afford it?
5. Will this job bring about a strain in my relationship with my friends or family members?

After considering the above questions in your mind, write down the answers. Now ask the pendulum,

"Should I take job A?" note the swing.

"Will there be any problems?" note the swing.

"Will I be satisfied?" note the swing.

"Will it help my financial growth?" note the swing.

"Will it help my career growth?" note the swing.

Also to be understood here is the Heisenberg Uncertainty Principle which says that the observer himself affects the observed in the experiment.

Earlier in the book we have understood that atomic particles can exist both as waves or as particles hence the experimenter has to decide in advance what he wants to see. In other words, it is impossible to separate the observer from the experiment.

It is advisable to dowse alone. Scientists define reality as something which can be touched, felt, seen, smelt and heard or else it should move a needle on the dial of an instrument. Pendulum works beyond physical dimensions that only a mind can get attuned to. Our minds get attuned to higher energies if we are searching for answers and are determined to find it. Love for a particular energy attunes us by spiritual practises like meditations and deep hypnosis or even something very simple as aiming or working towards being a simple and a humble human being.

"Wisdom is all there, catch it if you can".

Our conscious mind always leans towards the past and forms concepts based on our past experiences, learning and instances. All the time we are engaged in the futile activity of judging people. The *Bible* says, "Judge ye Not". It is a waste of time to judge people because then we will not have time to love them. As a healer this would be my earnest advice not to judge people because by doing so we are creating blocks for ourselves.

Preconceived concepts will also affect dowsing. We have seen that all the answers come from the unconscious mind and any preconceived notion would only lead to the pendulum giving answers desired by us. The unconscious mind is so benevolent that is always craving to please us.

To further enumerate this, let us study the example of a young boy who is deeply in love with a girl. His parents introduce him to 2-3 other girls. These girls are unknown to him. If he asks the question to the pendulum regarding the girl whom he loves, "Should I get married to...?" In all probabilities it will answer 'yes' because the boy has the preconceived notion of marrying the girl he loves.

"Expectation affects the outcome".

The *Bible* says, "You cannot enter the kingdom of Heaven unless you are a child". Hence be childlike and not childish. The attitude while dowsing needs to be that of innocence, full of curiosity and openness, devoid of any bias. This is the key to receiving answers from the pendulum.

To get correct answers, dowsing sequence needs to be followed and this is explained later on. If one goes as per the chain of sequence explained, one is most likely to achieve 95 per cent correct answers.

Dowsing Sequence

Man fools himself by praying for long life and subsequently fearing old age and death.

- Chinese Proverb

By now you would have understood how subtle the art of dowsing is and the various factors which affect its performance. Hence it is very important to follow the steps in dowsing to get good results.

Step 1: (Before starting dowsing) Affirm mentally or verbalise, "I choose to be in integrity of the overall mission. I revoke invitation to all manifestations such as those that are inconsistent to this. So it is now."

"I raise my level of integrity, wholeness and frequency and that of the pendulum to the highest limit today. So it is now."

Step 2 : (Before starting dowsing) Affirm and ask the pendulum, "I would like to dowse..." (name, situation, etc).

"Can I? "(To check whether you have skill)

"May I? "(To ask permission)

"Am I ready." (To tune into the frequency)

If you get 'Yes' for all the questions then proceed. If you get a 'No' for even one of the questions stop dowsing.

Step 3: Ask the question (after all logical approaches explained before)

Step 4: Affirm, "I wonder what is the answer "(3 – 4 times). This stops the unconscious mind from giving any preconceived answers as explained earlier. If you feel you have preconceived answer affirm, "Illusion break (3 minutes), ignore attachment".

Step 5: Note the answer.

Step 6: Ask, "Is this the truth?"

This question gives one more chance to the unconscious mind to give you correct answers. Note the swing.

Step 7: If pendulum gives feeble swing affirm, "Magnify swing".

Please note that all 5th dimension work is only by affirmation and positive thoughts, "As you sow so you shall reap".

Please remember dowsing cannot be used for personal greed and where it offends the rule of the game.

You will get what you deserve not what you desire.

-Baba

Suppose you dowse to know the outcome of a cricket match most likely it gives wrong answers due to preconceived concepts and also it offends the rule of the game. You are not supposed to know.

"Past is history, future is a mystery, present is a gift." Learn to be in the present because being in the present is a gift of existence.

Meditation helps one to be in the present and look at things as they are, without prejudice.

In case we use the pendulum for greed or for something not within the gamut of integrity, the pendulum goes dead and does not answer any questions. If this happens, ask the pendulum, "Are you dead" and if it says, "Yes" then do the following sequence of affirmation.

"I acknowledge relationship break down."

"I apologise for not being responsible."

"I ask to be forgiven."

"Please return to the original relationship."

"I invoke beings, spirit and seeds of dowsing to be implanted in the pendulum."

"Please restore this pendulum to original configuration. So it is now, so it is now, so it is now."

Do not let anyone touch your pendulum as they can deprogramme the pendulum with certain symbols.

It is very important to form a profound relationship with your pendulum. Never doubt it nor work with prejudice. In the *Gita,* Lord Krishna says, *"Shradda Van Labte Gyanam"*, meaning the more you have faith in me different will be the understanding.

Please remember the subconscious mind's first or most important task is to protect your interest.

Uses of Dowsing in Daily Life

Metaphor is halfway between the unintelligible and the common place.

-Aristotle

Dowsing has multiple uses right from finding application in the engineering to medicine, apart from water divining too. I shall enlist some very interesting uses for day-to-day application. The sequences covered in detail earlier need to be followed strictly.

1) Tracing a lost article:

Pendulum swing needs to be observed minutely, and for this it is essential to understand and master 'Leading Edge Concept'. Pendulum swings more towards one direction than other side of mean position. If

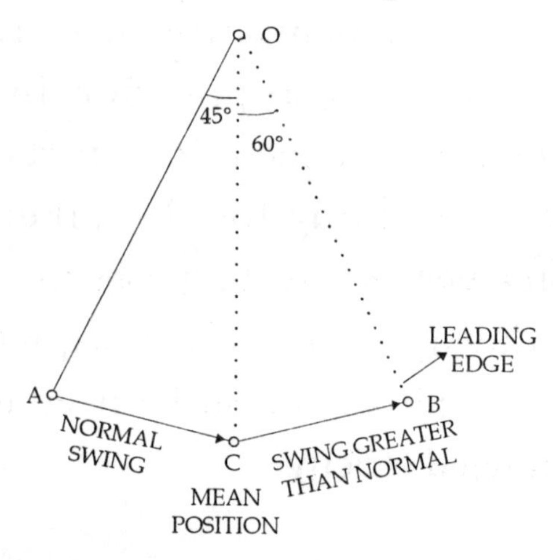

you observe the figure given you will note that the angle COB is greater than angle COA. This is known as the Leading Edge.

To try this out, ask the pendulum "Show me the east". Stand facing the north and you will see that the pendulum comes to a mean position and then swings more on the east rather than on the west side. You may proceed with other questions you need to ask only after you are absolutely sure of the answer to the first one.

If you have lost or misplaced an article in the house, follow the sequence detailed below.

The questions to be asked, "Will I find it?" Note the swing. "Is it in this room?" (The room in which you are dowsing). Note the swing. Then ask about other rooms in the house. Till you get a positive answer continue asking for the exact place. The moment you get a 'Yes' answer, go into further details. "Is it in my cupboard?" Note the answer. "Is it in my drawer?" Note the swing.

"Is it in my shelf?" Proceed till you get the correct answer with respect to the place. Keep noting the swing. You will definitely be able to locate the place where the object is.

2) Finding the lost object inside a room:

Once you know the place where the object is, it may still be difficult to find it. In such a situation use another method called 'Triangulation Method'.

Ask first, "Is the object in front of me?" Note the swing.

If 'No', then ask, "Is the object behind me?" Note the swing.

If 'No', ask, "Is the object to my right?" Note the swing.

If 'No', ask, "Is the object to my left?" Note the swing.

If it still gives a 'No', answer, then ask, "Is the object in this room?" Generally there will be no contradiction.

Now go to position A as shown below and ask, "Is the object in front of me?" if it is 'Yes' then draw an imaginary line in front of you.

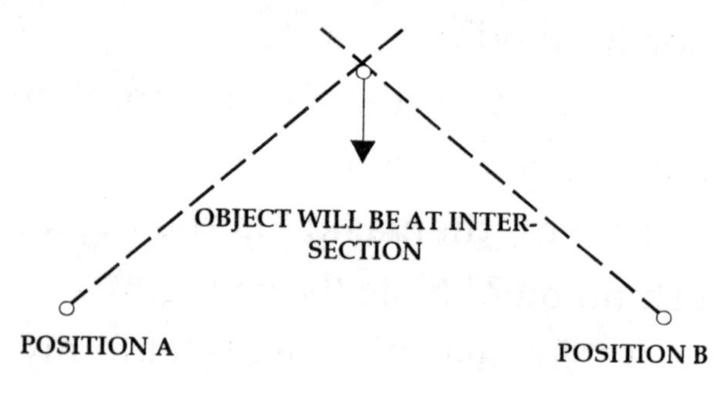

Now stand on position B and repeat the question and draw an imaginary line as shown above and you will be glad to find the object at the intersection of these two imaginary lines.

3) Finding lost people:

In case this unfortunate event happens to anyone, the pendulum is your best friend.

First ask the whereabouts of the person, where he/she was last seen with. Keep on probing further with the help of the pendulum and with your own intelligence. This process will help you narrow down probabilities. Again do not have preconceived ideas or prejudices.

Caution: Pendulum does not replace the normal legal assistance

from police. However, a pendulum will help even the police to narrow down the innumerable options and thus make the hunt much easier. You should be in an absolutely balanced state of mind to dowse and any kind of irritation, worry or anxiety may yield wrong results. If you are not sure of dowsing for family members then request your friend dowser to do it for you.

4) Selecting a lifepartner:

Supposing one receives marriage proposals from 3-4 persons with equal status, qualification and good looks, then it becomes difficult to make a selection. Once again you need to understand that any preconceived idea will not give a correct answer. In case you are in love with one of them then the pendulum will give a "Yes" answer when asked questions pertaining to that person.

Ask logical questions like, "Can we make successful life partners?" rather than, "Will we be happily married?" One would agree that making a marriage work successfully is in the hands of the couple.

5) Selecting a business partner:

Selecting a good business partner is as important as selecting a life partner, as one can become a king or a pauper depending upon whom you select. Human beings are big actors always wearing a mask. What they appear to look cannot portray what they actually are from within.

I was personally a victim twice by selecting two partners – one of them with technical ability, and the other with financial ability but selection of both of them proved to be a disaster. Both the companies sank into oblivion within an year of establishment. Since I was not a master of dowsing at that time it took a lot of time and money to set right the damages caused.

One has to be very careful in selecting business partners due to various factors like:

- Understanding ability,
- Skills like technical, administration, marketing, communication, etc.
- Financial capabilities.
- Demarcation of work.
- Health of the partner.
- General demeanour of the person, viz., if he is a nosey type,

egoistic, stubborn about his point of view and not flexible, etc. These are the details to be looked into or else there is bound to be many problems in any business venture whether small or big.

A pendulum can be used to select the partners by asking questions like:

- "Can I have partnership with Mr so and so?"
- "Can I expect cooperation at all levels from him?"
- "Should I proceed immediately?"

  "If 'No' after 6 months, 12 months, so on.

Generally very close friends and relatives should be avoided in partnership due to various other socio-economic reasons.

(6) Planning business expansion: Once I met a friend at one of the Rotary meetings and upon asking how he was faring on the business front, he said, "I run a small scale industry with big scale problems." Most of the SSI units get into problems due to over expansion and speculation without scientific projection and adequate planning of cash flows. Margins are squeezed and payments are differed so they land up only paying interest to bankers or finance corporations for life having pledged the personal properties. I have seen people becoming bankrupt due to poor business sense and greed to become rich overnight.

There is no formula for instant richness. A total trust in god and your own intelligence and intuition are the best aids in producing good results. First talk to people in similar line of business and ask them to narrate their experiences and difficulties. Some may give you genuine advice whereas others may even confuse you so that you do not become their competitor. Framing of appropriate questions to friends and the use of pendulum could prove extremely beneficial. You could ask:

"Is this expansion/ diversification necessary?"

If so, "Can I expect to earn more out of it?"

If so, "Can I expect to earn Rs 10,000/- and above?"

If so, "Can I expect to earn Rs 20,000/- and above?"

If so, "Can I expect to earn Rs 30,000/- and above?"

Till the pendulum gives 'No' swing you can keep asking for the correct answer.

If the final inference meets your requirement only then there is any point in diversification, if one is going to earn only Rs 5000/- per month after investing Rs 50 lakhs then it does not make any good business sense.

(7) Selecting real estate:

Sometimes purchase of land or house or already existing property lands us in a delusion. While some of the properties could bring innumerable good fortune, others may not be very lucky.

We will cover Vastu related aspects in the subsequent chapters to give more insight into energy work.

First check the documents with the pendulum.

"Are these documents original and authentic?" If yes, only then proceed.

"Can I purchase this property?"

"Can I expect prosperity after obtaining this property?"

"Are there any misappropriate or disqualified energies in the property?"

If it is yes then find the location with the pendulum either on map or at site itself.

(8) Selecting proper diet:

"You are what you eat" is an old adage. Food makes us or breaks us. Everybody is different due to his or her constitution. Food affects our thoughts and thoughts create emotions which in turn leads to action. Emotion is energy in motion that stays put in different parts of our body creating various diseases and disorders.

If you are health conscious and would like to live a disease-free life please make a detailed list of foods that you usually have for breakfast, lunch, dinner, etc., including coffee/ tea, alcohol, desserts, etc.

Now ask the pendulum to give 'yes' swing for foods agreeable to your constitution and 'no' swing for those not agreeable. Keep moving the pendulum down the list and check the items that are compatible. You can comfortably discontinue all those items that are rejected by the pendulum because it has done so for your highest good.

(9) Selecting proper investments:

Before making any investment in shares, debentures or private firms take the help of the pendulum to make safe and beneficial investments. Place the catalogue or the name of the company under consideration for investing under the pendulum and ask the pendulum,

"Is this company worth considering for investment?"

"Will my investment be safe?"

If the pendulum swings to the yes position then ask, "Can I expect profits from this investment?"

If the pendulum swings to the yes position, "Can I expect good returns in the future too?"

Finally, "Are you sure if I invest in this company I will not lose my investment?"

Dowsing for Therapeutic Use and Healing

God heals and doctor sends the bill.

-Mark Twain

Healing the human body is one of the most complicated and fascinating subjects as it is very difficult for anyone to pinpoint the reason for a disease. Human beings are not a single physical body as we perceive but a soul with physical, emotional, mental and spiritual body represented by seven psychic chakras and seven auras around them which is bioplasmic body or the fourth state of matter. Anything wrong with our chakras and auras directly reflects on our physical body. For example, one may be physically very fit but emotionally not well-balanced, i.e., he/she may be a short-tempered person. Such an imbalance could also cause a physical problem. Hence it is very important to balance our four bodies by following a certain discipline mentioned below:

Physical body: Yoga, aerobics, jogging, massage.

Emotional body: Practising regular meditation and abstaining from constant negative thinking patterns.

Mental body: Focusing by practising Trataka and following breathing pattern by being aware of breath.

Spiritual body: Being in constant awareness that you are a divine soul yourself and everything that is being experienced is only a divine experience. The *Gita* says, *"Atmo Vid Sukhomo Tarthi"*. One who knows he has divine consciousness has no sorrow in life.

We suffer due to reasons like:

1. Improper lifestyle

2. Improper diet
3. Genetic reasons
4. Karmic reasons
5. Negative thought pattern
6. Bad environment
7. Addictions
8. Lack of fresh air and exercise

We indulge in keeping awake for late hours in the night and wake up late in the morning causing a lot of physical damage to our body because our body is biologically conditioned to wake up well before sunrise. Moreover, one can benefit innumerably from the early morning sunshine which is full of positive and healthy energy very much essential to keep us fit during the whole day.

Proper diet is very important and vegetarian diet is the best. However, non-vegetarian food taken in limited quantity from protein point of view is acceptable. Eating habits are a matter of personal choice. Diet should consist more of fruits, leafy vegetables, greens, sprouts, juices, oats, plenty of water, dry fruits, yoghurt, butter, milk, wheat grass.

Organically processed vegetables are preferred. One must cut down the use of refined sugar, sweets, concentrated salt, aerated drinks, ice-creams, desserts, cooked tomatoes, chips and popcorns.

The genes inherited by us from our parents are the genetic reasons for the hereditary diseases such as diabetes, heart-related ailments. However, solution is now available for such diseases in Holistic and Alternative Medical Sciences. Holistic science considers the human body as a whole, hence the name "Holistic" has evolved since it is timeless (*Sanathana*) and is the most natural way of living. All therapies like yoga, ayurveda, reiki, pranic healing, magnetotherapy, acupressure, pyramidology, aroma-therapy, massage, Bach flower remedies have solutions for present day problems of mankind because most of the diseases are due to stress and wrong lifestyles. Moreover, adopting the alternative therapy is not very expensive and are easy to practice too and have virtually no side effects at all.

Karma is nothing but Newton's 3rd law of motion which is "Every action has an equal and opposite reaction".

The *Bible* says, "Whatever you sow is what you reap".

Baba says, "Good deeds will always get you good results and bad deeds will never get you good results". Karma is different from fate as karma is due to our own actions, deeds, speech, words and even thought. Hence wrong thought process also leads to bad karma. One may start to think God is vindictive it is not so, every disease is a divine surgery teaching us to come back to normalcy, provided we set aside our ego and learn from the disease.

A bad working environment and residence in a bad locality also affects the human psyche greatly. Occupational hazards and safety have to be also taken into account especially in factories. If we constantly inhale fumes we are bound to get lung-related diseases. Addiction to smoking, alcohol, drugs, tobacco, tea and coffee also lead to diseases. Hypnosis and NLP (Neuro Linguistic Programming) work very well for deaddictions.

Man's mind is the most evil thing ever created. In fact, god has created heaven on earth but it is the human mind that has made it evil. Due to bad behaviour like hurting someone physically and mentally, depriving someone of their childhood, unfair business practice all lead to human misery in the long run.

"Healing means return to the state of happiness."

Use of Pendulum for Healing

(1) For scanning chakras:

Human body takes in *prana* or the life force through the seven psychic chakras and any blockage in them results in ill health.

Make the patient (person to be healed) lie down and give instructions to the pendulum.

"Give me clockwise swing if chakra is functioning properly and anti-clockwise swing if the chakra is blocked".

Bring the pendulum from the base chakra upwards upto the crown chakra after passing it through sacral, solar plexus, heart, throat and brow chakras. At each chakra, pause for a minute and note the reading of your pendulum. Repeat the same by making the person lie on his stomach and check the back chakras. Observe the chakras that are indicating blockages carefully.

For example, if the pendulum gives an anti-clockwise swing for root, solar plexus and throat, it is an indication that the person has anxiety for survival related issues like money, house, career, fulfillment of ambition, etc., while also suppressing something in speech (not communicative).

Next take the pendulum to one of the above mentioned three chakras and ask, "Is it 50 per cent blocked?" Note the swing for 'yes' and 'no'. If the answer is 'no', then ask, "Is it 60 per cent blocked?" Note the swing. Ask, "Is it 70 per cent blocked?" Note the swing and so on.

You will be able to arrive at the exact percentage of blockage. Cleanse the chakras by pranic, reiki, acupressure, etc., techniques and again check the percentage of the opening of chakras.

(2) Selecting proper treatment method:

There are many treatments available including sympathy. The patient tends to get confused as to which branch of science will suit him best. We live our life based on the suggestions given by others because everyone we meet has a different opinion. No science can claim to be a panacea for ills is the fundamental principle one must understand. The pendulum can be of great help here.

One can draw a chart as below:

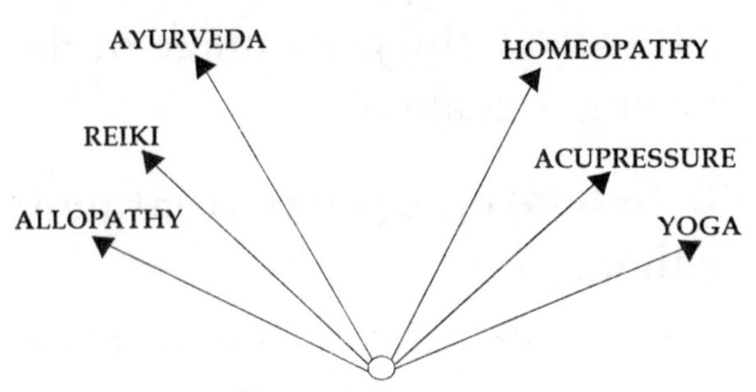

We could ask the pendulum, "Which of the healing sciences would best suit the person?" The pendulum would swing exactly on the lines indicated and not between them.

(3) Selecting homeopathy/Bach flower remedies

Homeopathy and Bach flower have one peculiar problem of

offering 3 – 4 remedies for the same diseases or disorder and it becomes difficult for the best homeopath to select a proper drug that would suit the constitution of the patient. Again a pendulum can be a great aid here.

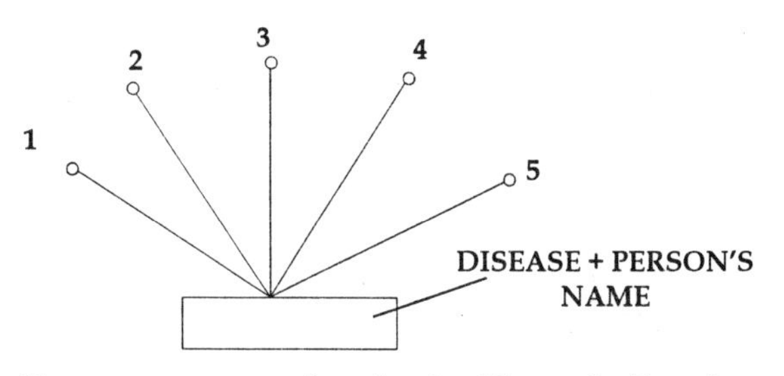

Even potency can be checked by a similar chart after short-listing from the above method.

Example : Swelling Problem

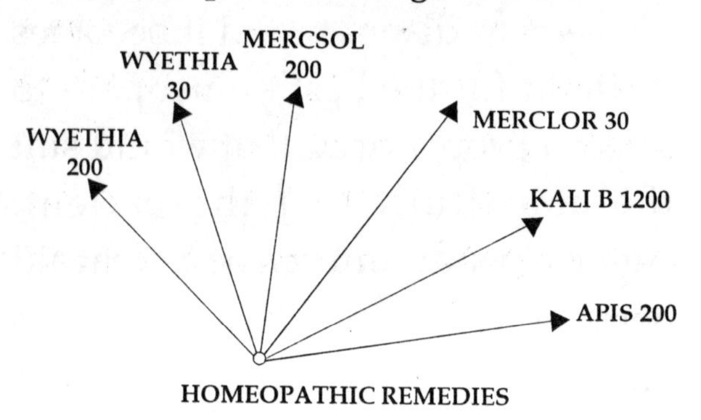

Example : Bach Flower For Depression

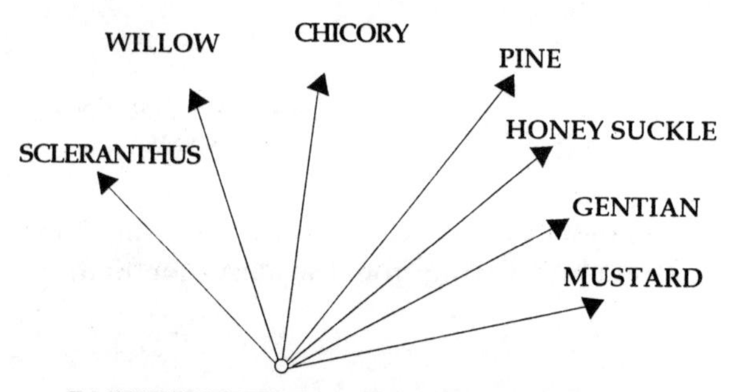

Dowsing for Fun

Be in this world as if you were a stranger or a traveller.

-Holy Koran

Dowsing can also be used for fun and relaxation apart from its day-to-day uses and therapeutic applications. It is a good tool for students also.

First, let us take the 0 to 180 chart as shown in the next page which has multiple applications. Take a protractor from a geometry box and draw the chart as shown and place the pendulum at the centre. This same chart can be used for 100 to 1,000, 1,000, to 10,000, 10,000 to 100,000 and so on.

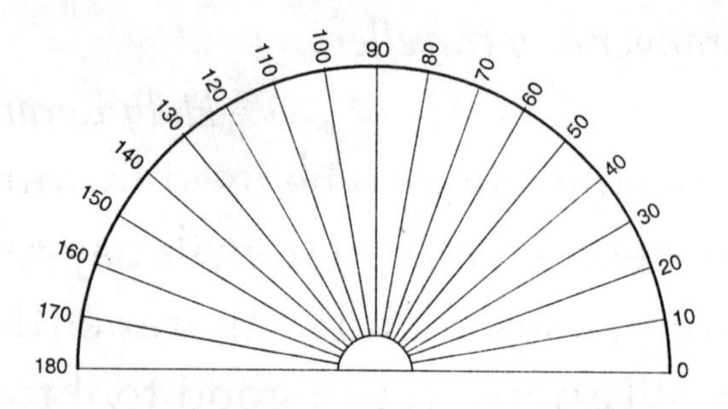

The above chart is to be read from right to left, on purpose, to extract information from the right side of the brain or subconscious mind and intuitive levels.

1. Dowsing for temperature : Ask the pendulum,

"What is the atmospheric temperature in centigrade now?"

"What will be the atmospheric temperature in centigrade tomorrow?"

"What will be the normal temperature of the human body in the morning?"

"What is my body temperature now?"

"What is temperature in centigrade inside my fridge?"

Again reconfirm by, "Is it the truth?"

2. Dowsing for birth time/date:

In astrology, birth date and time are the most important thing and any mistake or uncertainty would change the entire horoscope and may become 'horrorscope' for some.

Write down the probable dates of birth for the person whom you are dowsing along with the time of birth showing in A.M./P.M. clearly one below the other as shown below:

25th July 1961
24th July 1961
23rd July 1961
22nd July 1961

7.05 P.M.
7.10 P.M.
7.15 P.M.
7.20 P.M.

The 0 to 100 chart can also be used.

Bring the pendulum near each date and time separately one after the other and ask, "Is this correct?"

If 'No' then proceed to the next, if 'Yes' ask, "Is this the truth?"

Repeat it 4-5 times to confirm the exact date and time.

I have been successful in determining the correct time, date, day and year of birth for many of my clients with the help of dowsing.

3. Dowsing for personal questions:

There is nothing silly when you sit alone with a pendulum to dowse a few personal things for your personal life. First, make a proper list of questions and counter questions before you proceed.

Q.1: Which career change will suit me most?

Make a detailed list of change envisaged by you and check each with the pendulum.

Q.2: What will make my innermost identity happy?

List out your daily chores and things you are desirous of doing even as hobbies.

Q.3: Which part of my body needs focus?

Write down the part of the body and other health issues.

Q.4: If you are a bachelor or spinster wanting to know to which zodiac sign your better-half will belong to ask,

"Which zodiac sign person would suit me the most as my spouse?"

List all the people you have in mind. Again don't forget the sequence of steps to be taken.

Q.5: What line can I choose if I moonlight for extra income?

People have both professional career as well as obsessions that they like to convert into profession too and being unable to balance out the two they get into difficulties.

Q.6: Where should I go for next holiday?

List out all the holiday spots.

Q.7: How can I improve my relationship with... (person's name) for our mutual benefit?

List out all the possibilities.

Q.9: What duties and responsibilities on the work front, family and social levels needs to be addressed by me now?

List all the duties.

Q.10: What should I do for my spiritual growth?

List down all the possible areas.

Q.11: Which goals set by me needs to be focussed upon?

This is important because man pursues many goals and as a result achieves none. Dowsing will help man to focus on one goal.

Q.12: What can I do for the society? Which talent of mine will be useful to the society?

List out all the areas of your strength which one can be used to make you a better citizen.

4. Using dowsing for maps:

Take the world map preferably with longitudes and latitudes on it. Take the pendulum on one corner and ask, "Show me the direction of the largest oil reserve in the globe". When it shows, draw an imaginary line and then again take it to the other corner and repeat the question and the intersection of the two lines will be the largest oil reserve. Note down the coordinates and check the same with any book on facts and figures, the figures have to tally. Thus you can go on doing a lot of research on your globe for other natural things.

This can be extended to say a state map with longitudes and latitudes and question like, "Is there any oil reserve in row No. 1,2,3..." the pendulum will give a strong 'yes' swing where it finds the oil reserves.

This is a boon to diggers as lots of time can be saved by making use of dowsing techniques. However, physical check again at site is always beneficial.

5. Industrial application of dowsing:

Pendulum is also a useful tool for the engineers because they are often caught between 2-3 options for the same problem.

Let us take an example of taking a decision to change the heat exchanger used for cooling machines. Under such circumstance, the engineer can ask the pendulum the following questions,

(a) "Is the heat exchanger functioning normally?" Note the swing.

(b) "Is it scaled by deposits?" Note the swing.

(c) "If so, does it require cleaning?"

(d) "Is the quality of water that is being fed to the exchanger good?"

(e) If not, list out various options of treating the water and select the most economical and technically feasible option.

(f) "Is the quality of oil used suitable?"

(g) "Is the temperature rise within permissible limits?"

This will reduce your shut down time to a great extent saving money for the company. One can be innovative in the usage of the pendulum for tricky answers. Sometimes scientific answers are not available and we need to do some trial and error. However, let me emphasise once again that the pendulum does not replace the normal scientific tests and procedures.

6. Dowsing for household appliances:

Dowsing can also be used for any trouble-shooting problems with appliances like television, refrigerator, microwave, airconditioner, audio player, car, etc.

Trouble-shooting guidelines are given in most of the manuals but some of them are so complicated that a layman finds it rather confusing to attend to the emergencies and takes recourse in the nearest service centre.

If you have the diagram of the appliance in the manual the pendulum will give strong swings in the area of a problem by programming, "Give me a clockwise swing when you reach the part which is out of order."

Sometime the problem is so simple like a fuse getting burnt or some such thing that it could take little time to rectify and probably it could be attended by simple means.

Even when we take the appliance to a service centre generally they tend to charge exorbitantly for the spare parts that are replaced. Again the pendulum can check the defect and the rates quoted by the company.

Water Divining Using Dowsing

The world is a garden, the Lord its gardener, Cherishing all, none neglected.

-Adi Granth

Water is the most precious gift given by god to man and hence it is aptly called the 'Nectar of Life' or technically 'Universal Solvent' as it dissolves everything. The higher energies knew that man could survive without food for some days, but not without water. Hence they gave special powers to some people who could locate underground water. These people came to be known as 'Water Diviners'.

Every diviner looked not just for water alone but water of good potable quality known as Juvenile water source. Juvenile water is neither recycled water, nor is it the collection from rain, but it is formed due to various chemical reactions and is sourced from the depth of the earth. This water is the best source of potable quality. A reaction of an acid (HCL) with a base (NaoH) will produce salt (Nacl) and water. This reaction is continuously going on inside the earth's core. This watery by-product turns to steam which moves rapidly away from the heat and as steam expands it finds cracks in the mantle of the earth and emerges as mineral springs or geysers.

The most famous geysers on the earth are in the Yellow Stone Park, USA, that has therapeutic qualities of healing many skin diseases. Some wells near holy places also have such waters and they are rich in mineral content. Some of these wells are well-known in West Bengal and Tamil Nadu for having cured people mysteriously of their vague disorders. In Maldives, drinking water at the mosques are from such wells. Water has a very special importance in all the religions and this is evident from the extensive use of water in the religious rituals.

Juvenile water is never a part of the water table and is usually non-polluted by effluents and toxic substances. It is this source of water that a dowser looks for and such a water is called 'Good vein of water'. These veins are found between a depth of 50 to 250 feet and anything beyond 400 feet is considered to be a waste of time.

Nature gives its own clues for juvenile water sources like ants build anthills on cross section of veins of water. Wild bees locate hives over these sources and may even swarm above them. Animals like dogs, snakes and other underground nesting animals have their home near such sources. If you have a pet at home notice that they spend maximum time around their favourite places in the house and for all you know those must be serving the juvenile source below.

Some trees and plants will also take roots from such source like juniper, daisies, rings of mushrooms and hardwood trees.

To start dowsing for water the steps are as follows:

First declare to the pendulum your desire, viz.,

- "I want to dowse for juvenile source of water, can I, may I, am I ready?"
- If the answer is 'Yes', proceed further.
- "Is there a juvenile source of water below the place you are dowsing?"
- If 'Yes', "Show me the direction of the vein."

  Use leading edge principle to notice the vein.
- "Are there one, two or three veins...?"

  If 'Yes', ask, "Show me the intersection of these veins."

  As you walk in the direction pointed by the pendulum, the

pendulum will start rotating in elliptical orbit strongly. Stand over it and ask, "Am I standing on the intersection of the vein." If 'Yes', proceed further.

- "Is this juvenile source less than 250 feet deep?"
- If 'Yes', "Will it yield at least 5 gals/ minute of water?"
- If 'Yes', "Is it of good potable quality?"
- If 'Yes', "Does it have a good taste?"
- If 'Yes', "Does it have any toxic element in it?"
- If 'No', "Is it at less than 50 ft, 100ft, 150 ft, 200 ft, 250 ft?" and so on to determine the depth.

You can also use 0-100 chart explained earlier, changing it for 100-200, 200-300ft and so on.

- Next step is to check the yield, start with 1 gal/min, 2 gal/min, 3 gals... by asking, "Will it yield... gals per minute of water?" Again you could use 0-100 chart by changing it to 0-10 gals per minute.
- Ask, "Is it the truth?"
- Again standing over the spot ask, "Is this the best place to drill?"

A general word of caution here is that water divining should be attempted after about 5-6 months of rigorous practice . Your practice of dowsing should constantly be 85 per cent right answer before you even think of water divining. You must maintain a diary of all dowsing done by you for yourself and others detailing even the date, day, time and tick mark those which have come true so that you can check your own dowsing abilities. Water dowsing can also be done for large areas by using contour plans or area plans divided into rows and columns and numbering each box and finally checking the findings physically at site.

Energy Ley Lines and Power Centres

The infinite is the source of joy, there is no joy in the finite. Only in the infinite is there joy. Ask to know the infinite.

-Upanishad 7.23

Energy ley lines are natural flow of cosmic energy that are of positive sign. They come down to the earth at places which we call power centres.

These power centres have domes which are placed where water rises vertically through the earth's strata. Water veins are generated here when water flows at different levels where the strata has cracks or where there are soft inclusions. So all the water flows away from the center of a dome formation. Where a water dome and energy ley come together we call it power center. Water is of negative sign. Therefore at power centers both positive and negative energies are balanced, i.e., both yin and yang are present. These are acupuncture points of the earth.

In fact, all religious places, pyramids, churches, public meeting places were built on such sites before Renaissance because when energies are balanced one feels comfortable and a sense of well-being prevails.

We all know that ultimately it is the balance of energy which is important. Excess of neither positive nor negative energy is not advisable. We all have both these energies within us and harmony is only possible by meditation, yogic practises and through arts like Reiki that always help you to be in balance. This is medically known as "Homeostatis".

If one lives in an environment with imbalance of energies, it is possible that one would fall sick. This is the reason for the focus attention received by sciences viz., Vastu, Fengshui, Pyramidology, Crystal and other forms esoteric sciences.

Everything in this universe or biosphere has its own energy and vibrates at its own frequency.

A dowser can now easily tune himself to these frequency to find more answers. He can dowse a house for locating any negative or noxious energy coming from any article present in the house and thus that imbalanced energy could either be balanced by adopting rectification method or removed from the house.

All holy places have ley lines and hence when one approaches them, right attitude is required as it can be a good learning experience. Six to eight foot wide beams of yang energy can run like meridians or capillaries all over the surface of the earth carrying nourishment in various forms to countryside and its inhabitants of the area.

On a sacred place stand and ask,

"Is there an energy ley line below?"

If 'Yes', "Show me the direction." Notice the same and follow the leading edge.

"Show me the downstream." Generally ley lines run like river which cross with juvenile water source and create sacred domes.

"Show me the direction of a sacred dome?" Notice the same and as you approach you may find your pendulum's elliptical orbit becoming stronger in speed of rotation and also you will feel tingling of hair at the base of your neck.

What do ley lines feel like?

Like water lines, a vertical field extends up from the ley line through homes and buildings. The nature of this field is yang or energetic. A person who sits or lies over a ley line for an extended period of time will tend to be hyperactive. This can work to advantage in healing or in situations where extra energy is useful, but if someone is already very energetic then the ley line may cause an unhealthy situation. And if the ley line is negative, the negative aspects of extra energy will be manifest in tension, anxiety, and neurosis.

What do water lines feel like?

As water flows through underground streams, it creates a subtle electromagnetic field, several feet wide that rises vertically above the water line, even through multiple floors and stories. This vertical planar field of electro-magnetic energy affects people physically, mentally and spiritually.

It is one thing to experience the effect of a water line by standing over it for a short time. It is another thing to work or sleep over a water line. A water line has a yin or passive field, associated with it. Being on a water line will tend to slow you down and make you feel lazy or apathetic. People who work at desks over water lines often have problems getting enough energy to get work done or even to get started.

Water lines can have serious negative effects when the water line is polluted physically, or psychically. Negative water lines not only create a state of passivity but can be detrimental to one's physical and mental health. I consider negative water lines to be one of the world's major causes of disease.

Where does the power centre lie?

Ley lines and water lines have fundamental similarities and differences. They both form a network of force fields over our planet and seem to affect human behaviour, although in different ways. Ley line originate from outside the earth, while water springs originate from inside the earth. Ley lines travel in straight tracks with 90° turns, while water lines are non-linear and circuitous.

The power of an ancient monument sites lies in the interaction of the telluric earth field of southwest United States.

This feeling of power as sensed by our consciousness and body is the key thing to seek at any sacred place – it is the effect of the field on our consciousness that really counts, not the name, technicalities or details.

When you visit ancient monuments or sacred places of any

kind, be aware of and experience your level of consciousness. Feel how your mood changes, what kinds of thoughts you experience. If you have negative feelings or don't feel a place is safe or right, avoid it.

Ancient monuments are a blessing because they elegantly mark power centres. In many parts of the world, all you have to do is find a megalithic monument, mound or ceremonial place and this would mean that you have found an important power centre.

If you want to find a power centre and there is no monument or ancient place near you what would you do? Currently, there are two ways of finding power centres. One is just to be able to feel them naturally. I have one friend who can just walk to a power centre and say, "Here it is". People like this, though, are quite rare. The other way to find power centres and earth energies is through the technique of dowsing.

Frequently asked Questions on Dowsing

Whenever something is new it is ridiculed, then fought for and then finally accepted. This has been the sequence of all major discoveries and inventions. Sometimes it has so happened that eminent scientists have been enemies of scientists themselves. People believe in things that they may not know because it is something to know things and another thing to believe in it. Dowsing was also ridiculed by sceptics for the simple reason that they did not know anything about it.

Probably the best solution could be to present such people with books on dowsing that could clarify their doubts or they could attend our "Psychic Healing Course" which clarifies all the doubts on this wonderful science that has inert potentials.

For the benefit of readers and practising dowsers some questions are listed below for enhancement of their further knowledge.

Who can dowse?

Everyone is born with this capability. Children up to the age of

15 to 16 are almost universally sensitive. It has been established that in a group of 25 adults two to five will obtain the dowsing reaction immediately, if properly instructed. Others may have to practice for a while before they manifest what seems to be a birthright talent.

Those who discover they can dowse stand on the threshold of new and challenging experiences. Dowsing normally begins on sources of underground flowing water. As your interest grows you may find yourself putting in many hours of practice. Other targets may present themselves as success follows success.

How can I tell if I am a dowser?

Try one of the basic devices. Hold it in the search position and walk forward, keeping the mind focused on your potential target, i.e., underground flowing water. If you feel you have covered too much ground or passed over a known target without result, try one of the other devices. Remember that with a little practice and some patience nearly everyone can achieve a dowsing reaction. As with all human skill aptitude will vary. We believe, however, that dowsing is a basic ability and that familiarisation with it is a simple matter for old and young alike.

Which device shall I start with?

Angle rods will respond to most people on the very first attempt. You can make them from metal stock, preferably ⅛ to 3/16 inch in diameter and from 18 to 30 inches long. Bend two rods at a point approximately 6 inches from the ends to form a right angle "grip". Hold the rods at waist level pointing forward like two pistols. As you walk forward, mentally ask for whatever it is that you seek. The rods will swivel, either crossing inward or diverging outward, as you pass over the target. As you pass beyond it, they should resume their original position.

The forked stick, however, may suit you just as well. It is also called Y-rod. It has an age-old connection with dowsing. Simply cut a fork about 18 to 20 inches long and ⅛ to ¼ inch in diameter, from a tree or bush. It should be limber enough to be responsive when the two ends are held in a palms up position, yet stiff enough to resist all but a definite pull from a vertical, or search position. Proceed as with the angle rods, mentally holding the desired target until the forked stick reacts over it by a pulling motion. This may be towards or away from the body although many dowsers find the latter response to be the norm. You may want to try forked sticks made of metal or plastic.

Pendulum could be tried by the beginners too. Anything of ¼ to ½ ounce weight such as a ring will serve. Secure it to a six inch string or chain. Hold the string or chain between the thumb and forefinger about two to four inches above the suspended weight. Position it above your right knee and set in motion.

The wand or bobber is another device and can be made from a four foot branch of a tree, stripped of leaves and shoots and about ½ and ¼ inch in diameter. A similar length of rigid wire or the plastic tip of a fishing rod will also serve. Grasp the wand close to the smaller end and set it in motion, either vertically or horizontally, as you walk over the target area, the opposite motion or a circular motion will prevail and signal you that your search has been a success.

Dowsing is more than dowsing for water...

Did you know that there are many applications for dowsing? Dowsing for water is an important application of dowsing, however, dowsing is not limited to water, search or location. There are many other aspects including dowsing for minerals, dowsing for electro-magnetic fields, noxious rays and geopathic zones, dowsing for lost objects, dowsing for lost person, dowsing for personal-related subjects, spiritual dowsing, dowsing and the immune system—the list goes on and on. The applications are endless.

What is map dowsing?

The following explanation of map dowsing is given by the American Society of Dowsers. With a map or a sample sketch of the terrain, an individual property, whether a house less than an acre in a size or a ranch of several hundred square miles, all these could be dowsed by one proficient in this method. Map dowsing is best performed not with Y or L rods but with a pendulum. One way is to overlay the map with a grid dividing it into rectangles (though this grid can be mentally pictured or imagined). The dowser then asks which rectangle(s) on the grid will contain the best site(s) for drilling a water well. The pendulum will give the answer.

Are there any scientific studies of water dowsing?

Yes there are several. A recent study of water dowsing in arid regions was published by the journal of scientific exploration.

Is there any particular time for dowsing?

Any time is fine but as explained earlier being a divination tool the best time is early morning or after your prayers. We can use a pendulum anytime of the day without any restrictions. One may keep in mind that dowsing should not be done in waxing and waning moon days due to its direct effect on the psyche.

In which places should the pendulum be restricted in usage?

As explained earlier, due to the sanctity of dowsing, it should not be used in toilets or touched with dirty hands or after eating. Best is to store the pendulum in the place of worship such as your prayer room or the place generally used for offering prayers. Crystal pendulum picks up both positive and negative energies almost instantaneously. Similarly one should not dowse near electronic gadgets like computers, television, microwave ovens, cell phones as they all work at high frequency and may affect the results on dowsing.

How much time does it take to be confident of its use?

As explained earlier this is in your own hands. You should keep a diary of events that have been dowsed for by you and how many have reached the status of actually happening. These facts and figures will only give you confidence. It is purely a subjective and not an objective reality. You must get 85 per cent correct answers before you dowse for complicated stuff.

How to get best results from a pendulum?

Pendulum works on our state of mind, so please do not attempt to dowse when you are angry, anxious, irritable and expecting results in your favours. It is not possible for any human being to be in a 100 per cent perfect state of mind all the time and hence suggestions given earlier require to be followed strictly. If you know self-hypnosis, go into hypnosis and come out after five minutes and then dowse, it will give good results.